MISSA PAPAE MARCELLI

FOR

SIX VOICES

BY

PALESTRINA

EDITED AND ARRANGED FOR MODERN USE

BY

HENRY WASHINGTON

Duration of performance 30 minutes

Chester Music

PREFACE

The whole plan of singing in musical modes shall be constituted not to give empty pleasure to the ear, but in such a way that the words may be clearly understood by all, and the hearts of the listeners be drawn to the desire of heavenly harmonies, in the contemplation of the joys of the blessed. **Extract from a canon of the Council of Trent, 1562.**

If not supreme among Palestrina's one hundred and more settings of the Mass, *Missa Papae Marcelli* is certainly unique. Its peculiar qualities of textual clarity, spiritual joy, rhythmic vitality and harmonic resource, though reflected abundantly in later Masses, were never again to be so perfectly combined, so consistently maintained. It is also unique in that it bears a dedicatory title. Marcellus II reigned for three weeks only in the Spring of 1555, when Palestrina had lately been appointed to membership of the Pontifical Choir. It is on record that the Pope was dismayed by perfunctory singing in the Papal chapel during the celebration of the Good Friday liturgy. Summoning the singers to his presence, he enjoined on them that " whatever was performed on those holy days when the mysteries of the Passion and Death of the Saviour were celebrated, must be sung in a suitable manner, with properly modulated voices, and so that everything could be both heard and understood properly." The Abbé Baini, Palestrina's over-imaginative biographer, gives an impressive account—long discredited—of the Roman master's producing this Mass ten years later (in 1565) before a commission of cardinals, as convincing proof that polyphonic music could be composed without prejudice to a clear declamation of the text. Baini then suggests that by this single act Palestrina saved the art of sacred polyphony from total censure. But, though the Mass was not printed until 1567, it is now known that it was composed at a much earlier date, even before the memorable admonition of Pope Marcellus. Nevertheless, it complied fully with the Tridentine directives, thus showing a notable departure from the composer's less mature style of *cantus firmus* and canonic writing in which intelligibility of words was often sacrificed to contrapuntal ingenuity.

The two known originals of the complete work are a copy in choirbook form at Santa Maria Maggiore and another copy at the Capella Sistina. Both contain the seven-part Agnus Dei II and both are without title and author's name. The Mass was first printed during Palestrina's lifetime in his Second Book of Masses (1567), bearing the title—by which the above-mentioned exemplars were identified—but not including the second Agnus Dei. Two copies of this publication are in the British Museum,* and I have made careful reference to them in the preparation of the present edition while accepting Haberl's transcription of 1892 for the second Agnus Dei. The many modern editions of *Missa Papae Marcelli* reflect its widespread popularity at the present time, not least in the Eternal city in whose basilicas it first resounded. That it was no less popular in Palestrina's day may be inferred from the fact that Giovanni Anerio and Francesco Soriano both published arrangements of it, the one for four voices, the other for eight. There is a twelve-part adaptation in the archives of the Chiesa Nuova, St. Philip's Oratory in Rome.

A number of present-day editions of this famous work appear to have been copied one from the other, thus perpetuating a few minor inaccuracies and a considerable amount of clumsy word-placing. In this new edition I have been at pains to devise a smooth underlaying of the Latin text in conformity with the rules laid down in Palestrina's lifetime by Zarlino and Vicentino. Certain melodic constructions demand elision of

* K.9.a.7 and Hirsch III. 973, 1-3.

the final E in the words *Kyrie* and *Christe.* Where this occurs the silent E is printed in italics. Sixteenth-century note-values have been halved to accord with later acceptance of the crotchet as the normal unit of time. Palestrina's accidentals are printed in the usual position, i.e. to the left of the note affected while other accidentals, restricted to a minimal application of the theory of *musica ficta,* appear in small type above the note. A short vertical stroke above or below a note is added where necessary to assist the singer in defending verbal rhythm against the accentual power associated with the modern bar-line and to define the true agogic rhythm where an original long note has been replaced by two tied notes of shorter duration. The slur is used solely to denote a ligature in the original notation.

Written in the Hypoionian mode with the *chiavette* this music lies rather high in the natural pitch and is here transposed a whole tone lower. It will bear further downward transposition to the extent of a fourth from the original pitch. In this case Cantus and Altus could be sung by altos and tenors respectively. The seven-part Agnus Dei II incorporates a canon three-in-one and the voices concerned may be allowed to stand out from the general texture. The first resolution is given to Altus II (replacing Tenor I) and though the voice-range of the new part is identical with the remaining single Tenor, any redundant first tenors who take over the second Altus will find the *tessitura* appreciably higher.

Missa Papae Marcelli is usually classed with Palestrina's very few freely-composed Masses, though many efforts have been made to identify its motifs with various Gregorian chant formulae, and even with the fifteenth-century folksong *L'homme armé.* A few years before the publication of the Mass in 1557, a decree of the Council of Trent had forbidden the use of secular themes in the composition of music for the Sacred liturgy. It is true, nevertheless, that every section of *L'homme armé*, broadly paraphrased, can be discerned in the main themes of this Mass. Palestrina had a *penchant* for subtle allusion in the spiritual and musical order; if, indeed, he used the title *Missa Papae Marcelli* to disguise a third setting of *Missa L'homme armé* it would be time to ascribe to him a virtue hitherto unsuspected—a dry sense of humour!

HENRY WASHINGTON.

THE ORATORY,
LONDON,
September, 1963.

MISSA PAPAE MARCELLI

PALESTRINA
Edited by
HENRY WASHINGTON

KYRIE

15
-son, Ký - ri - e e - léi - son, Ký-rie e - léi -
-son, Ký - ri - e e-léi - son, Ký - rie e-léi - son,e -
son,Ký-rie e - léi - son, Ký-rie e -
-son, Ký - ri - e e - léi - son, Ký - ri - e
Ký - rie e léi - - son,Ký - ri - e e-léi - son, Ký - rie
-son, Ký - rie e léi - son, e-léi - son,Ký - rie e - léi -
20
-son,Ký-rie e - léi - - son.
-léi - son, Ký-rie e-léi - - - son.
-léi - son, e - léi - son, Ky - rie e-léi - - son
e-léi - - son, Ký - ri - e e-léi - son.
e - léi - son, Ký-rie e-léi - son, e - léi - son.
-son, Ký-rie e - léi - son, Ký - rie e - léi - son.
allargando

25
30
Chrí - ste e - léi - son, Chrí - ste e -
Chrí - ste e - léi - son, Chrí - ste e - léi -
Chrí - ste e - léi -
Chrí - ste e -
Chrí - ste e - lêi - son, Chrí -
Chrí - ste e - léi -
p Soli
35
-léi - son, Chrí - ste e - léi - son,
-son, Chrí - ste e - léi - son, Chrí -
-son, Chrí - ste e - léi - son, Chrí - ste e -
-léi - son, Chrí - ste e - léi - son, Chrí - ste e - léi -
-ste e - léi - son, Chrí - ste e - lei - son,
-son, Chrí - ste e - léi - son, Chrí - ste e -

40
Chrí - ste e - léi - son, e-léi - son, Chrí -
-ste e-léi - son, Chrí - ste e - léi - son, Chrí - ste e-
léi - - son, e - léi - son, Chrí-ste e - - léi - son,
- son, Chrí - ste e - léi - son, Chrí - ste e-léi - son, Chrí-
Chrí - ste e - léi - - son, Chrí - ste e -
- léi - - son, Chrí - ste e-léi - son,
cresc.
dim.
45
50
-ste e-léi - son, Chrí - ste e - léi - - son.
-leí - son, e - léi - son, Chrí - ste e - léi - son.
Chrí - ste e - léi - - - - son.
- ste e - léi - son, Chrí - ste e - léi - son.
- léi - son, Chrí - ste e-léi - son.
Chrí - ste e - léi - son, e - léi - son.
allargando

55
Ký - rie e - léi - - son, Ký - rie e - léi -
Ký - rie e - léi - - - - son, Ký -
Ký - rie e - léi - son, Ký - rie
Ký - rie e - léi -
Ký - rie e -
Ký - rie e - léi - son, Ký - rie e - léi -
f Tutti
60
- - - son, Ký - rie e léi - son,
- rie e - léi - - son, Ký - rie e - léi -
e - léi-son, Ký - rie e - léi - - son, Ký - ri -
- - - son, e - léi - - son, Ký
-léi - - son, e - léi - son, Ky - rie e -
son, Ký - rie e - léi - -

65
70
Ký - rie e - léi - - - - son, Ký-rie e -
-son, Ký - ri - e e - léi - - son, Ký-rie e - léi - son,
-e e - léi - son, Ký - ri - e e - léi-son, Ký - ri - e
- rie e - léi - son, Ký-rie e - léi - - son, Ký -
léi - - son, Ký-rie e - léi -
-son, Ký-rie e - léi - - - - son,
75
-léi - - son, e - léi - - - son.
Ký-rie e - léi - son, Ký-rie e - léi - son, Ký - rie e - léi - son.
e - léi-son, Ký - rie e - léi - - son.
-rie e - léi - - - son, Ký - rie e - léi - - son.
- - son, e - léi - son, Ký - rie e-léi - son.
Ký-rie e - léi - son, e - léi - son.
allargando

GLORIA

CANTUS
ALTUS
TENOR I
TENOR II
BASSUS I
BASSUS II
Reductio Partiturae
5
Et in ter - ra pax ho-mí - ni - bus bo - nae vo -
Et in ter - ra paxho - mí - ni - bus bo - nae vo -
Bo - nae vo -
Et in ter - ra pax ho - mí-ni - bus
Bo - nae vo -
Et in ter - ra pax ho-mí - ni - bus
♩= 126
mf Tutti
10
-lun-tá - tis. Lau - dá - mus te. Be - ne - dí-ci-mus te.
-lu - tá - tis. Lau - dá - mus te. Be - ne - dí-ci-mus te.
-lun-tá - tis. Be - ne - dí-ci-mus te. Ad - o -
Lau - dá - mus te. Ad - o -
-lun-tá - tis. Be - ne - dí-ci-mus te.
Lau - dá - mus te. Ad - o -
f
p Soli
mf Tutti

15
Glo - ri - fi - cá - mus te. Grá - ti - as á - gi -
Glo - ri - fi - cá - mus te. Grá - ti - as á - gi -
-rá - mus te. Grá - ti - as á - gi -
-rá - mus te. Glo - ri - fi - cá - mus te. Grá - ti - as á - gi -
Glo - ri - fi - cá - mus te.
-rá - mus te. Grá - ti - as á - gi -
poco rit.
a tempo
Soli
f Tutti
20
-mus ti - bi pro - pter ma - gnam gló - ri - am tu - am.
-mus ti - bi tu - am Dó -
-mus ti - bi Dó -
-mus ti - bi pro - pter ma - gnam gló - ri - am tu - am.
pro - pter ma - gnam gló - ri - am tu - am. Dó -
-mus ti - bi Dó -
mf

25
30
De - us Pa - ter o - - mní - po -
-mi - ne De - us, Rex cæ - lé - stis.
-mi - ne De - us, Rex cæ lé - stis.
De - us Pa - ter o - mní - po -
-mi - ne De - us, Rex De - us Pa - ter o - mní - po -
-mi - ne De - us, Rex cæ lé - stis.
p
35
-tens. Dó - mi - ne Fi - li, Dó - mi - ne Fi - li u - ni -
Dó - mi - ne Fi - li, Dó - mi - ne Fi - li u-nigé -
Dó - mi - ne Fi - li, Dó - mi - ne Fi - li u - ni -
-tens. Dó - mi - ne Fi - li u - ni -
-tens. Dó - mi - ne Fi - li
Dó - mi - ne Fi - li, Dó - mi - ne Fi - li u - ni -
mf
f

40
-gé-ni-te, u - ni-gé-ni - te Je - su Chri - ste, Je -
- ni-te, u - ni-gé-ni - te Je - su Chri - ste, Je -
-gé - - ni - te Je - su Chri - ste, Je -
-gé-ni-te Je - su Chri - ste, Je -
u - ni-gé-ni - te Je -
-gé-ni-te Je - su Chri - ste, Je -
p
f
45
- su Chri - ste. Dó -
- su Chri - ste. Dó-mi-ne De - us, A-gnus De - i,
- su Chri - ste. Dó-mi-ne De - us, A - gnus De - i,
- su Chri - ste. A - gnus De - i, Dó -
- su Chri - ste. Dó-mi-ne De - us, A - gnus De - i,
- su Chri - ste. Dó -
p
mf

50
-mi-ne De - us, A - gnus De - i, Fí - li - us Pa - - -
Fí - li - us Pa - tris,
A - gnus De - i, Fí - li - us Pa -
-mi-ne De - us, A-gnus De - i,
Fí - li - us Pa - -
-mi-ne De - us, A - gnus De - i,
55
60
-tris, Fí - li - us Pa - - - tris.
Fí - li - us Pa - tris, Fí - li - us Pa - tris.
-tris, Fí - li - us Pa - - tris, Pa - - - tris.
Fí - li - us Pa - tris, Fí - li - us Pa - tris.
-tris, Fí - li - us Pa - - - tris.
Fí - li - us Pa - tris, Fí - li - us Pa - tris.
ritardando

65
Qui tol - lis pec - cá - ta mun - di, mi -
Qui tol - lis pec - cá - ta mun - di, mi - se - ré - re no -
Qui tol - lis pec - cá - ta mun - di, no - bis, mi -
Mi - se - ré - re no - bis.
Qui tol - lis pec - cá - ta mun - di, mi -
Mi - se - ré - re no - bis.
Meno mosso
mf Soli
p
70
- se - ré - re no - bis. Qui tol - lis pec - cá - ta mun - di,
- bis, no - bis. Qui tol - lis pec - cá - ta mun - di,
- se - ré - re no - bis. Qui tol - lis pec - cá - ta mun - di,
Qui tol - lis pec - cá - ta mun - di,
- se - ré - re no - bis.
Qui tol - lis pec - cá - ta mun - di,
mf Tutti

75
sú - sci - pe, sú - - - sci - pe de - pre - ca - ti - ó - nem
sú - sci - pe, sú - sci - pe de - pre - ca - ti - ó - nem
sú - sci - pe, sú - sci - pe de - pre - ca - ti - ó-nem no -
sú - sci - pe, sú - - sci - pe
sú - sci - pe, sú - sci - pe de pre - ca - ti - ó - nem
sú - sci - pe, sú - sci - pe
f
mf
80
no - stram, de - pre - ca - ti - ó - nem no - stram. Qui se - des ad
no - stram, de - pre - ca - ti - ó - nem no - stram.
- - stram. Qui se - des
de - pre - ca - ti - ó-nem no - stram.
no - stram. Qui se - des ad
de - pre - ca - ti - ó - nem no - stram.
p Soli
mf Tutti

85
déx-te - ram Pa - tris, mi - se - ré -
Mi - se - ré - re no - - - bis.
ad déx-te - ram Pa - tris, mi - se - ré -
Mi - se - ré - re no - - bis.
déx-te - ram Pa - tris, mi - se - ré -
Mi - se - ré - re no - - bis.
p Soli
p
90
95
- re no - - bis. Quó - ni - am tu so - lus san - ctus. Tu
no - bis. Quó - ni - am tu so-lus san - ctus.
- re no - - - bis. Tu so -
Quó - ni - am tu so - lus san - ctus. Tu so -
- re no - - bis. Tu so -
Quó - ni - am tu so - lus san - ctus.
Tempo primo
f Tutti
Soli

100
so - lus Dó - - mi - nus.
Tu so - lus Al - tís - si -
- lus Dó - - mi - nus. Al - tís - si -
- lus Dó - - mi - nus. Tu so - lus Al - tís - si -
- lus Dó - - mi - nus.
Tu so - lus Al - tís - si -
Tutti
105
Je - su Chri - ste, Je - su Chri -
- mus, Je - su Chri - ste, Je - su Chri -
- mus, Je - su Chri - ste, Je - su Chri -
- mus, Je - su Chri - ste, Je - su Chri -
Je - su Chri - ste, Je - su Chri -
- mus, Je - su Chri - ste, Je - su Chri -
f
p

110
-ste. Cum San-cto Spí - ri - tu, in gló - ri - a,
-ste. Cum San-cto Spí - ri - tu. De -
-ste. Cum San-cto Spí - ri - tu, in gló - ri - a De -
-ste. Cum San-cto Spí - ri - tu, cum San-cto Spí - ri - tu,
-ste. Cum San-cto Spí - ri - tu, in gló - ri - a De -
-ste. Cum San-cto Spí - ri - tu,
mf Soli
115
in gló - ri - a De - i Pa -
- i Pa - tris, A - - men, De - i Pa -
- i Pa - tris, A - - men,
in gló - ri - a De - i Pa - tris,
- i Pa - tris, A - - men, in gló - ri - a,
in gló - ri - a De - i Pa -
mf Tutti

120
-tris, A - - men, in gló - ri - a, in gló - ri - a De - i Pa -
-tris, A - - - men, in gló - ri - a De - i Pa -
in gló - ri - a De - i Pa -
A - - - men, in gló - ri - a De - i Pa -
in gló - ri - a De - i Pa -
-tris, A - - - men, in gló - ri - a.
125
-tris, A - - men.
-tris, A - men, A - - - men.
-tris, A-men, A - - - - men.
-tris, A - - men.
-tris, A - men, A - - - - men.
A - - - - men.
allargando

CREDO

CANTUS
ALTUS
TENOR I
TENOR II
BASSUS I
BASSUS II
Reductio Partiturae
♩= 116
mf Tutti
p
mf
5
10
Pa - trem o - mni - - - po - tén - - - tem,
Pa - trem o - mni - - - po - tén - - - tem, fa - ctó - rem
Pa - trem o - mni - - - po - tén - - - tem, fa - ctó - rem
fa - ctó - rem
Pa - trem o - mni - - - po - tén - - - tem,
fa - ctó - rem
vi - si - bí - li - um ó - mni - um, et in -
cæ - li et ter - ræ, vi - si - bí - li - um ó - mni - um.
cæ - li et ter - - - ræ, et in -
cæ - li et ter - - ræ, vi - si - bí - li - um ó - mni - um.
vi - si - bí - li - um ó - - - mni - -
cæ - li et ter - - ræ, vi - si - bí - li - um ó - mni - um, et in -

15
-vi - si - bí - li - um. Et in u - num Dó-mi - num, et in u - num Dó -
Et in u - num Dó - mi - num,
-vi - si - bí - li - um. Et in u - num Dó -
Et in u - num Dó - mi - num, et in u - num Dó -
-um. Et in u - num Dó - mi - num.
vi - si - bí - li - um. Et in u - num Dó -
mf
20
- mi - num Je - sum Chri - stum. Et
Fí - li - um De - i u - ni - gé - ni - tum. Et
- mi - num Je - sum Chri - stum, Fí - li - um De - i u - ni - gé - ni - tum.
- mi - num Je - sum Chri - stum. Et
Fí - li - um De - i u - ni - gé - ni - tum. Et
- mi - num Je - sum Chri - stum. Et
p
mf

25
ex Pa-tre na - tum an - te ó-mni - a sǽ - cu - la. De - um de
ex Pa-tre na - tum an - te ó-mni - a sǽ - cu - la. De - um de
De - um de
ex Pa-tre na - tum an - te ó-mni - a sǽ - cu - la.
ex Pa-tre na - tum. De - um de
ex Pa-tre na - tum an - te ó-mni - a sǽ - cu - la.
f
30
De - o, De - um ve - rum, De - um ve - rum de De - o
De - o, lu - men de lú-mi - ne, De - um ve - rum
De - o, lu - men de lú-mi - ne, De - um ve - rum
Lu - men de lú-mi - ne, De - um ve - rum, De - um ve - rum de De - o
De - o, De - um ve - rum de De - o
Lu - men de lú-mi - ne, De - um ve - rum
p
f
p
f

35
40
ve - - - - - ro. Gé - ni - tum, non fa - ctum, con -
de De - o ve - ro. Gé - ni - tum, non fa - ctum,
de De - o ve - - - ro. Gé - ni - tum, non fa - ctum, con -
ve - ro, de De - o ve - ro. Con -
ve - ro. Gé - ni - tum, non fa - ctum,
de De - o ve - - - - ro. Con -
mf
45
- sub - stan - ti - á - lem Pa - - tri: per quem ó - mni - a fa - cta
per quem ó - mni - a fa - cta sunt.
- sub - stan - ti - á - lem Pa - - tri: per quem ó - mni - a fa - cta
- sub - stan - ti - á - lem, per quem ó - mni - a fa - cta sunt.
per quem ó - mni - a fa - cta sunt.
- sub - stan - ti - á - lem Pa - - tri: per quem ó - mni - a fa - cta
f

50
sunt. Et pro-pter no-stram sa - lú -
Et pro-pter no-stram sa - lú - tem
sunt. Qui pro-pter nos hó - - - mi - nes, et pro-pter no-stram sa - lú -
Qui pro-pter nos hó - - - mi - nes,
Qui pro-pter nos hó - - - mi - nes,
sunt. Et pro-pter no-stram sa - lú -
p
mf
55
-tem de - scén - dit de - cæ - lis.
de-scén-dit de cæ - lis, de - scén - dit de cæ - - lis.
-tem de - scén-dit de cæ - lis.
de - scén - dit de cæ - lis, de-scén-dit de cæ - lis.
de-scén - dit de cæ - lis.
-tem de - scén - dit de cæ - lis.
ritardando

60
65
Et in-car-ná-tus est de Spí-ri-tu San-cto ex Ma-rí-a
Et in-car-ná-tus est de Spí-ri-tu San-cto ex Ma-rí-a Vír-
Et in-car-ná-tus est de Spí-ri-tu San-cto ex Ma-rí-a
Et in-car-ná-tus est ex Ma-rí-a
Et in-car-ná-tus est ex Ma-rí-a
Et in-car-ná-tus est de Spí-ri-tu San-cto.
Meno mosso
p
mf
70
Vír-gi-ne: Et ho-mo fa-ctus est.
-gi-ne: Et ho-mo fa-ctus est.
Vír-gi-ne: Et ho-mo fa-ctus est.
Vír-gi-ne: Et ho-mo fa-ctus est.
Vír-gi-ne: Et ho-mo fa-ctus est.
Et ho-mo fa-ctus est.
p
poco rit.

CANTUS
ALTUS
TENOR
BASSUS
Reductio Partiturae
75
80
Sub Pón-ti - o Pi - lá - - -
É - ti - am pro no - bis: sub Pón-ti - o Pi - lá - - -
Cru - ci - fí - xus é - ti - am pro no - bis: sub Pón-ti - o Pi - lá -
Cru - ci - fí - xus é - ti - am pro no - bis:
L'istesso tempo
p Soli
85
-to pas - sus, et se - púl - tus est. Et re - sur - ré - xit tér - ti -
-to pas - sus, et se - púl - tus est. Et re - sur - ré - xit tér - ti-
-to pas - sus, et se - púl - tus est. Et re - sur - ré - xit tér - ti-
pas - sus, et se - púl - tus est. Et re - sur - ré - xit.
rit.
A Tempo primo
p
mf
90
-a di - e. Et a - scén - dit in cæ - lum:
-a di - e. Et a - scén - dit in cæ - lum:
-a di - e, se - cún - dum Scri - ptú - - ras. Et a - scén - dit in cæ - lum: se -
Se - cún - dum Scri - ptú - - - ras. Et a - scén - dit in cæ - lum.
mf

95
100
se - det ad déx - te - ram Pa - - tris. Cum gló - ri -
se - det ad déx - te - ram Pa - - tris. Et í - te - rum ven - tú - rus est cum gló - ri -
- det ad déx - te - ram Pa - - tris. Et í - te - rum ven - tú - rus est.
Et í - te - rum ven - tú - rus est.
p
105
- a, ju - di - cá - re vi - vos et mór - tu - os:
- a, ju - di - cá - re vi - vos et mór - tu - os: cu - jus re - gni non e - rit
Vi - vos et mór - tu - os: cu - jus re - gni non e - rit
Ju - di - cá - re vi - vos et mór - tu - os: cu - jus re - gni non e - rit
p
110
115
cu - jus re - gni non e - rit fi - nis, non e - rit fi - nis.
fi - nis, cu - jus re - gni non e - rit fi - nis, non e - rit fi - nis.
fi - nis, cu - jus re - gni non e - rit fi - - - - - nis.
fi - nis, cu - jus re - gni non e - rit fi - nis.
ritardando
mf
p

120
CANTUS
Et in Spí - ri - tum San - ctum Dó - mi - num,
ALTUS
Et in Spí - ri - tum San - ctum Dó - mi - num, et vi -
TENOR I
Et in Spí - ri - tum San - ctum Dó - mi-num, et vi - vi -
TENOR II
Et in Spí - ri - tum San - ctum Dó - mi - num, et vi -
BASSUS I
San - ctum Dó - mi - num,
BASSUS II
Et in Spí - ri - tum. Et vi -
A Tempo
Reductio Partiturae
mf Tutti
p
125
et vi - vi - fi - cán - tem: qui ex
-vi - fi - cán - tem, et vi - vi - fi - cán - tem: qui ex
-fi - cán - tem: qui ex
-vi - fi - cán - tem, et vi - vi - fi - cán - tem: qui ex Pa -
et vi - vi - fi - cán - tem: qui ex
-vi - fi - cán - tem: qui
mf
f

130
Pa - tre Fi - li - ó-que pro - cé - dit. Qui cum Pa -
Pa - tre Fi - li - ó-que pro - cé - - dit. Qui cum
Pa - tre Fi - - li - ó - - que. Qui cum Pa -
- - tre Fi - li - ó - que pro - cé - dit. Qui
Pa - tre Fi - li - ó - que pro - cé - dit.
ex Pa - tre Fi - li - o. Qui cum Pa -
p
135
-tre. Et con -
Pa - tre et Fí - li - o si - mul ad - o - rá - tur.
-tre et Fí - - li - o si - mul ad - o - rá - tur, et con -
cum Pa - tre et Fí - li - o si - mul ad - o - rá - tur, et con glo -
Si - mul ad - o - rá - tur.
- - tre et Fí - li - o. Et con -
mf
mf

140
- glo - ri - fi - cá - tur: qui ___ lo-cú - tus est per Pro-phé - - -
Qui ___ lo-cú - tus est per ___ Pro - phé -
- glo - ri - fi - cá - tur: qui ___ lo-cú - tus est per ___ Pro - phé -
- ri - fi-cá - tur: qui ___ lo-cú - tus est per ___ Pro-phé - -
Qui ___ lo-cú - tus est per ___ Pro-phé - tas. ___
- glo - ri - fi - cá - tur: qui ___ lo-cú - tus est per ___ Pro - phé -
f
145
150
- tas. Et u - nam san - ctam ca - thó - li - cam et a-po -
- tas. Et u-nam san - ctam ca - thó - li - cam et a-po-stó-li -
- tas. Et u-nam san - ctam ca-thó-li - cam et a-po-stó - li -
- tas. Et u - nam san - ctam ca-thó - li - cam et a - po -
___ Et u-nam san - ctam ca-thó - li - cam.
- tas. ___ Et a-po-stó-li -
p Soli
mf

. . . . and rising prices . . . .

165
-ca-tó - - - rum. Et ex - spé -
-tó - - - - rum. Et ex - spé - cto, et
-ca - tó - rum, pec - ca - tó rum. Et ex-spé - cto, et
pec - ca-tó - - rum. Et ex - spé -
-ca - tó - - - rum. Et
pec - ca - tó - rum. Et ex-spé -
p Soli
170
-cto, et ex-spé - cto re - sur - re-cti - ó - nem, re - sur-re-cti - ó -
ex-spé - - cto re - sur - re-cti - ó -
ex - spé - cto re - sur - re-cti - ó - nem mor-
-cto, et ex-spé - cto re-sur - re-cti - ó - nem, re-sur - re-cti - ó -
ex - spé - - cto re - sur - re-cti - ó -
cto, et ex-spé - cto re - sur - re-cti - ó - nem
mf

175
-nem mor - tu - ó - - rum. Et vi -
- - - nem mor - tu - ó - - rum. Et
- tu - ó - - rum. Et vi - tam ven -
-nem mor - tu - ó - rum, mor - tu - ó - rum. Et
-nem. Et vi -
mor - tu - ó - - - - rum.
Tutti
180
-tam ven - tú - ri saé - - cu - li, et vi -
vi - tam ven - tú - ri, et vi - tam ven - tú - - -
tú - ri saé - cu - li, et vi - tam ven -
vi - tam ven - tú - ri saé - cu - li, et vi - tam ven -
-tam ven - tú - ri saé - - cu - li.
Et vi - tam ven - tú -

185
190
-tamven-tú-ri saé - cu - li. A - men, A - men,
- ri saé - cu - li. A - men, A -
-tú - ri saé - cu - li. A - men, A -
-tú - ri saé - cu - li. A - men, A - men, A -
A - men, A - -
-ri saé - cu - li. A - men, A - men,
mf
cresc.
195
A - - - men, A - - - - men.
- men, A - men, A - - men.
- men, A - men, A - men, A - - men.
- men, A - - men.
-men, A - - men, A - - - men.
A - men, A - - - men.
allargando
f

SANCTUS

CANTUS
ALTUS
TENOR I
TENOR II
BASSUS I
BASSUS II
Reductio Partiturae
= 126
mf Tutti
5
10
San - - - ctus, San - - - ctus, San - - - - - -
San - - ctus, San - - ctus,San - ctus, San - ctus, San -
San - - ctus, San - - ctus, San - - - ctus, San -
San - ctus, San - ctus, San - ctus, San - ctus, San -
San - ctus, San - - - - - ctus, San - ctus,
San - - ctus, San - - - ctus, San -

15
-ctus, San - - - ctus
- - ctus, San - - ctus, Sán - - - -
- - ctus, San - ctus, San - - - - -
- ctus, San - - ctus, San - - -
San - ctus, San - - ctus, San - ctus, San -
- - - - - - ctus
20
Dó - mi - nus De - us Sá - ba - oth,
-ctus Dó - mi - nus De - us Sá - ba - oth,
-ctus Dó - mi - nus De - us Sa -
-ctus Dó - mi - nus De - - us,
-ctus
Dó - mi - nus De us Sá - ba - oth,
p

25
— Dó - mi - nus De - us Sá - - ba -
— Dó - mi - nus De - us Sá - -
- - ba - oth, Dó - mi -
Dó - mi - nus De - us Sá - - ba - oth,
Dó - mi - nus De - - us Sá - ba - oth,
— Dó - mi - nus De - us Sá - ba -
mf
30
- oth, Dó - mi - nus De - us Sá - -
- ba - oth, Dó - mi-nus De - us Sá -
-nus De - - us Sá - ba - oth, Sá -
Dó - mi-nus De - us Sá -
Dó - mi - nus De - us Sá -
- oth, Dó - mi - nus De - us Sá - ba - oth.
f

35
- - ba - oth. Ple - ni sunt cae -
- ba - oth. Ple - ni sunt cae - li et ter -
- - ba - oth. Ple - ni sunt cae - li et ter -
- ba - oth. Ple - ni sunt cae - li et ter - ra,
- ba - oth.
Ple - ni sunt cae - li et ter - - -
p
Semichorus
p
40
- li et ter - ra, ple - ni sunt cae -
- ra, ple - ni sunt cae - li et ter - ra, et ter - -
ra, ple - ni sunt cae - li et
ple - ni sunt cae - li et ter - ra, ple -
Ple - ni sunt cae - li et ter - - ra, ple - ni sunt
- ra, ple - ni sunt cae -

45
-li et ter - - ra gló - ri - a tu -
- - ra gló - ri - a tu - - a,
ter - - - ra gló - ri - a tu - -
-ni sunt cae - li et ter - ra
cae - li et ter - ra gló - ri - a tu - -
-li et ter - - - ra
p
p
50
-a, gló - ri - a tu -
gló - ri - a tu - - - -
-a gló - ri - a tu - a, gló - ri - a tu -
gló - ri - a tu - a, gló - ri - a
-a, gló - ri - a tu - - - - - -
gló - ri - a tu - a, gló - ri -
. . . . and more fine works are lost from the repertoire.

- - a, gló - ri - a tu -
- a, gló - ri - a tu - -
- a, gló - ri - a tu - a, gló - - ri - a
tu - a, gló - ri -
- a, gló - ri - a tu - a,
- a tu - - a, gló - ri - a
55
- a.
- a, gló - ri - a tu - - a.
tu - a.
- a tu - a, gló - ri - a tu - a.
gló - ri - a tu - - a.
tu - a, gló - ri - a tu - a.
ritardando

60
65
Ho - sán - na in ex - cél - sis, ho - sán -
Ho - sán - na in ex - cél - sis, ho - sán -
Ho - sán - na in
Ho - sán - na in ex - cél - sis, ho - sán - na in
Ho - sán - na in ex -
Ho - sán - na in ex - cél - - - sis,
a tempo
f Tutti
70
- na in ex - - - cél - sis, ho - sán -
- na in ex - cél - sis, ho - sán - na
ex - cél - - sis, in ex - cél - sis, ho - sán - na
ex - cél - - sis, ho - sán - na
- cél - sis, ho - sán - na in
ho - sán - na in ex -

75
-na in ex - cél - sis, ho - sán - na
in ex - cél - sis, ho - sán - na in ex -
— in ex - cél - sis, ho - sán - na
in ex - cél - sis, ho - sán - na
ex - cél - - sis,
-cél - sis, in ex - cél - - -
80
in ex - cél - sis, in ex-cél - - sis.
cél - - - - - - sis.
in ex - cél - sis, ex - cél - sis.
— in ex - cél - sis, ex-cél - - sis.
ho - sán - na in ex - cél - sis.
-sis, ho - sán - na in ex - cél - sis.
allargando

BENEDICTUS

5
CANTUS
ALTUS
TENOR I
TENOR II
Be - ne - dí - - - - - -
Be - ne - dí -
Be - ne - dí - - - - ctus,
Be - ne - dí -
♩ = 104
Reductio Partiturae
p Soli or Semichorus

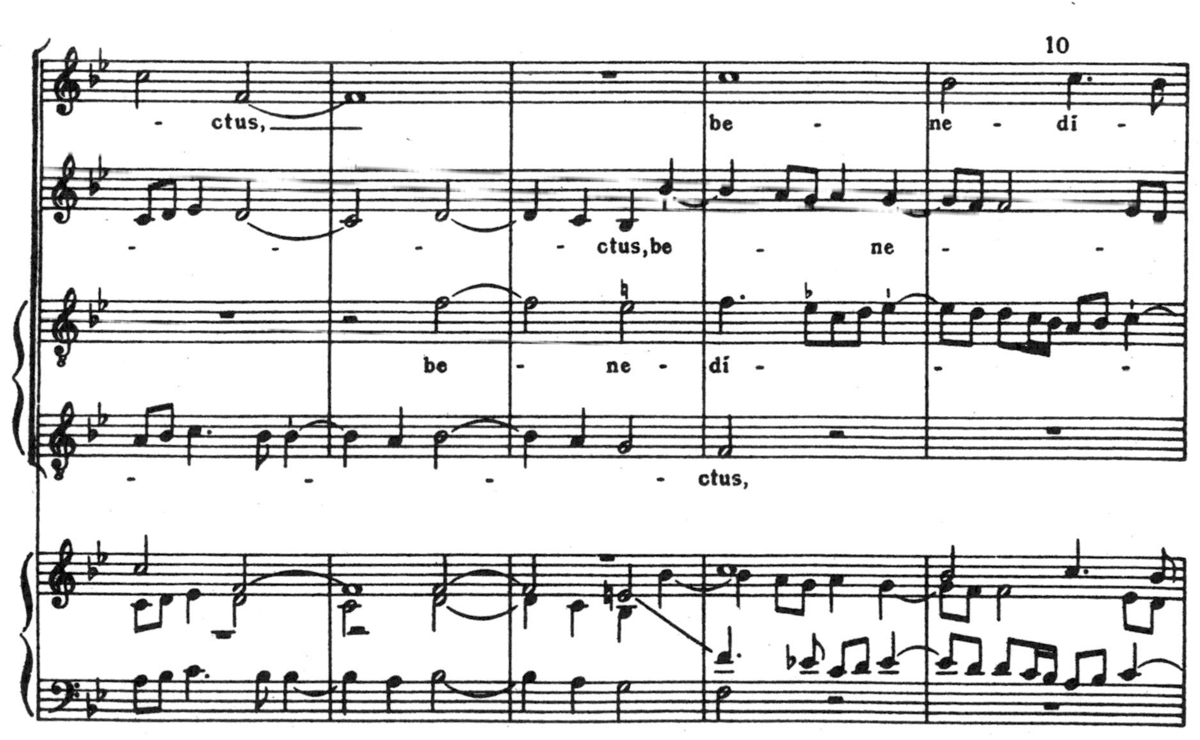
10
- ctus, be - ne - dí -
- - - - ctus, be - ne - -
be - ne - dí - - -
- - - - ctus,

15
ctus
dí - ctus, be - ne - dí - ctus
ctus qui ve -
be - ne - dí - ctus qui
20
qui ve - nit,
qui ve - nit, qui
nit, qui ve -
ve - nit, qui ve - nit,
25
qui ve - nit in
ve - nit in nó - mi-
nit, ve - nit
qui ve - nit, qui ve -
mf

30
nó - mi - ne Dó - - - mi - ni,
-ne Dó-mi - ni, Dó - - - mi - ni, in
in nó - mi - ne Dó - mi - ni, in nó - mi - ne Dó-mi -
-nit in nó - mi - ne
mf
35
in nó - mi - ne Dó - mi - ni, in nó - mi-ne Dó-mi -
nó - mi-ne Dó-mi - ni, in nó - mi - ne Dó-mi - ni, in nó-mi -
-ni, in nó - mi-ne Dó-mi - ni, in nó - mi-ne Dó -
Dó-mi - ni, Dó-mi - ni, in nó - mi-
40
-ni, in nó - mi - ne Dó - - mi - ni.
-ne Dó - mi - ni.
- - mi - ni, Dó - - mi - ni.
-ne Dó - - mi - ni.
ritardando

45
CANTUS
Ho - sán - na in ex - cél - sis, ho - sán - -
ALTUS
Ho - sán - na in ex - cél - sis, ho - sán - -
TENOR I
Ho - sán - na in
TENOR II
Ho - sán - na in ex - cél - sis, ho - sán - na in
BASSUS I
Ho - sán - na in ex -
BASSUS II
Ho - sán - na in ex - cél - - - sis,
♩ = 126
f Tutti
Reductio Partiturae
50
- na in ex - - - cél - sis, ho - sán -
- na in ex - cél - sis, ho - sán - na
ex - cél - sis, in ex - cél - sis, ho - sán - na
ex - cél - - - - sis, ho - sán - na
- cél - sis, ho - sán - na in
ho - sán - na in ex -

55
-na in ex - cél - sis, ho - sán - na
in ex - cél - sis, ho - sán - na in ex -
— in ex - cél - sis, ho - sán - na
in ex - - cél - sis, ho - sán - na
ex - cél - - - sis,
-cél - sis, in ex - cél - - -
60
in ex - cél - sis, in ex-cél - - sis.
-cél - - - - - - - sis.
in ex - cél - sis, ex - cél - sis.
— in ex - cél - sis, ex-cél - - sis.
ho - sán - na in ex - cél - sis.
-sis, ho - sán - na in ex - cél - sis.
allargando

AGNUS DEI I

CANTUS
ALTUS
TENOR I
TENOR II
BASSUS I
BASSUS II
Reductio Partiturae
5
A - gnus De - - - - i,
A - gnus De - - -
A - gnus De - - - - - -
A -
A - gnus De - - - - i,
♩ = 104
mf Tutti
10
A - gnus De - - - i, A -
- i, A - gnus De - i, A-gnus De -
- i, A - gnus De - - - i,
A - gnus De - - - -
gnus De - - - - i,
A - gnus

Photocopying inhibits publishing.

25
-lis pec - cá-ta mun - di, qui tol-lis pec - cá - ta mun -
qui tol - lis pec - cá-ta mun - - -
- ta mun - di, qui tol - lis - pec - cá - ta
- cá - ta mun - - - di,
- ta mun - di, pec - cá - ta mun - di,
qui tol - lis pec - cá - ta mun - -
mf
30
- - - di, qui tol - lis pec - cá - ta
- di, qui tol - lis pec - cá - ta mun - - -
mun - di, qui tol-lis pec - cá - ta mun - - -
qui tol - lis pec - cá - ta mun - - -
qui tol - lis pec - cá - ta mun -
- - di, qui tol - lis pec - cá - ta mun -
f
f
f

35
mun - di: mi - se-ré - re no - - bis,
- - di: mi - se - ré - re no - - - bis,
- di: mi - se - ré - re no - bis, mi - se -
- - di: mi - se - ré - re
- - - di: mi -
- - di: mi - se-ré - re no - - bis,
p
p
Soli p
p
40
mi - se - ré - re, mi - se - ré - re no - -
mi - se-ré-re no - bis, mi - se - ré -
re - re no - - - - - bis,
no - - bis,
mi - se - ré - re
- se - ré - re no - - bis,
mi - se - ré - re no -

45
- - - bis, mi - se - ré - re no -
- re no - bis, mi - se - ré - re no - - - - bis,
mi - se - ré - re no - bis, mi - se - ré - re no -
no - - bis, mi - se - ré - re no - bis, mi - se -
mi - se - ré - re no - - -
- - - bis, mi - se - ré - re
mf
mf
mf
50
- - bis, mi - se - ré - re no - bis.
mi - se - ré - re no - - - - bis.
- - bis. bis.
- ré - re no - - - - - - bis.
- - bis, mi - se - ré - re no - bis.
no - bis, mi - se - ré - re no - - bis.
ritardando

AGNUS DEI II

CANTUS I
CANTUS II
(Resolutio)
ALTUS I
ALTUS II
(Resolutio)
TENOR
BASSUS I
(Canon)
BASSUS II
REDUCTIO PARTITURAE
♩ = 104
Tutti
mf
5
A - gnus De - - - - i, A-gnus De - - - - - -
A - - - gnus De -
A - gnus De - i, A - - - gnus De - i, A - gnus Dé - -
A - - gnus De - - i, A - - gnus
A - gnus De - - - i, A - - gnus Dé - - i, A - gnus De -
A - gnus De - - i, A - - - gnus De - i, A - - gnus
A - - - gnus De - - i,

10

- - i, A-gnus De - - - - - -
- - - - i, A - gnus De - i,
- i, A - gnus De - - - - - i,
De - i, A - - gnus De - -
- - - - i, A-gnus De - - -
De - - i,
A-gnus De - -

15

i, qui tol - lis pec -
A - gnus De - i,
qui tol - lis pec - cá - ta mun-di, pec-cá - -
- i, qui tol - lis pec-cá -
- - i, qui tol - lis pec-cá - ta mun - di, pec-cá -
qui tol - lis pec-cá - ta mun - di,
- i, qui tol - lis pec-cá - ta mun - di, pec -

20
cá - - - - - - - - ta mun -
qui tol - lis pec - cá - ta mun -
- ta mun - - - di, mun -
- ta mun - di,
- - - - ta mun - - - - - di,
qui tol - lis pec - cá - ta
- cá - ta mun - di, pec - cá - ta mun -
25
- - - di, qui tol - lis pec - cá -
- di, qui tol - lis pec -
- - di, qui tol - lis pec - cá - ta mun -
qui tol - lis pec - cá - ta mun - - di:
pec - cá - ta mun - - di, qui tol - lis
mun - - di:
- di, qui tol - lis pec - - cá -

30
- ta mun - di: do - na no - bis pa - cem, do-
- cá - ta mun - - di:
- - - di: do - na no - bis pa-
do - na
pec - cá - ta mun - di: do - na no-bis pa -
do - na no - - bis pa - cem,
- ta mun - di: do - na no - bis pa - -
35
- na no - bis pa - cem, do - na no-bis pa -
do - na no - - bis pa -
- - - cem, do - na no - bis pa - - -
no - - bis pa - cem, do - na no-bis pa -
- - cem, do - na no - bis pa - cem, do-
do - na no - bis pa - cem,
- cem, do - na no - bispa - cem,

40

-cem, do - na nobis pa - cem, do -

-cem, do - na nobis pa - cem,

- - - cem, pa - - cem, do - na no-bis

-cem,

- na no-bis pa - - cem, do - na

do - na

do - na no - bis pa - - cem, do -

- - - na no - bis pa - - - -

pa - - - - - cem, do - - na

do - na no - bis pa -

no - - bis pa - - cem, do -

no - bis pa - - cem, do na no -

- na no-bis pa - cem, do - na no - bis

45
- cem, do - na no - bis pa - cem, do -
do - na no - bis pa - - -
no - bis pa - cem, do -
- - - cem, do - na no - - - - -
- na no - bis pa - cem, do - na no - bis
- - - bis pa - - - - - - -
pa - cem, pa - - - - - - -
50
- na no - bis pa - - - cem.
cem.
- na no - bis pa - - - cem.
- bis pa - - - - - - cem.
pa - cem, do - na no - bis pa - cem.
- cem, do - na no - bis pa - cem.
- cem, do - na no - bis pa - cem.
Allargando